The Meeting of Our Lord

from the series
The Twelve Great Feasts for Children

by Sister Elayne
with illustrations by Bonnie Gillis

CONCILIAR PRESS MINISTRIES
Ben Lomond, California

The Meeting of Our Lord
from *The Twelve Great Feasts for Children* series

Poems © copyright 2002 by Sister Elayne
Illustrations © copyright 2002 by Bonnie Gillis

All rights reserved.

Published by Conciliar Press Ministries, Inc.
P.O. Box 76
Ben Lomond, California 95005

Printed in China

ISBN 10: 1-888212-37-3
ISBN 13: 978-1-888212-37-2

The feast of the Meeting of Our Lord (also sometimes called the Presentation in the Temple) is celebrated on February 2

"Rejoice, O Virgin Theotokos, full of grace! From thee shone the Sun of Righteousness, Christ our God, enlightening those who sat in darkness! Rejoice and be glad, O righteous elder; thou didst accept in thine arms the Redeemer of our souls, who granteth us the Resurrection."

—*Troparion of the feast of the Meeting of Our Lord*

The prophet Simeon, in awe,
Looks at the One who gave the Law
To Moses, but who comes today
His own commandment to obey.

Then to the Mother of the Lord
He says, "A pain that's like a sword
Shall pierce thy heart, O blessed one—
To see the suff'rings of thy Son."

"For some shall love, but some shall hate
Thy Son, who in His mercy great,
Accepts from them His death so we
Can share His life eternally."

Be glad, then! For the Lord fulfills
His law for us of His own will
And with compassion
comes to seek
And heal the lame,
the sick, the weak.

Be glad! Be glad! For God on high
Becomes a Child to live and die

ABOUT THE AUTHOR AND ILLUSTRATOR:

Sister Elayne is a member of the community of St. Barbara Orthodox Monastery in Santa Barbara, California. Bonnie Gillis is an iconographer and illustrator. She currently lives in San Dimas, California, where she and her husband, Deacon Michael, attend St. Peter Antiochian Orthodox Church.

ABOUT THE SERIES:

In the Orthodox Church Year, the Feast of Feasts, in a class by itself, is the Resurrection. After the Resurrection in importance come the twelve Great Feasts. These feasts are the Church's celebration of, and participation in, key events leading to our salvation. The Great Feasts are commonly separated into Feasts of the Lord and Feasts of the Theotokos (the Mother of God).

Feasts of the Lord
Exaltation of the Cross
Nativity of Our Lord (Christmas)
Theophany of Our Lord (Epiphany)
Entry of Our Lord into Jerusalem (Palm Sunday)
Ascension of Our Lord
Pentecost
Transfiguration of Our Lord

Feasts of the Theotokos
Nativity of the Theotokos
Entry of the Theotokos into the Temple
Meeting of Our Lord (Presentation of Christ in the Temple)
Annunciation
Dormition of the Theotokos

In this series, we used simple verse and colorful illustrations to acquaint children with the themes and imagery of each of these feasts. We hope that this provides the children a groundwork for experiencing the joy and wonder of these truly Great Feasts.